THE WORLD'S TOP TENS

The World's Most
DANGEROUS
BUGS

by Nick Healy

Consultant:
Dr. Donald Lewis
Department of Entomology
Iowa State University
Ames, Iowa

Capstone
press
Mankato, Minnesota

Edge Books are published by Capstone Press,
151 Good Counsel Drive, P.O. Box 669, Mankato, Minnesota 56002.
www.capstonepress.com

Library of Congress Cataloging-in-Publication Data
Healy, Nick.
    The world's most dangerous bugs / by Nick Healy.
    p. cm. — (Edge books. The world's top tens)
    Summary: "Describes in countdown format 10 of the world's most dangerous
    bugs"—Provided by publisher.
    Includes bibliographical references and index.
    ISBN-13: 978-0-7368-5456-6 (hardcover)
    ISBN-10: 0-7368-5456-8 (hardcover)
    1. Insects—Juvenile literature. 2. Insect pests—Juvenile literature. 3. Poisonous
    arthropoda—Juvenile literature. I. Title. II. Series: The world's top tens
    (Mankato, Minn.)
    QL467.2H43 2006
    595.16'5—dc22   2005019423

Editorial Credits
Angie Kaelberer, editor; Kate Opseth, set designer; Jenny Bergstrom, book designer;
    Kelly Garvin, photo researcher/photo editor

Photo Credits
Bruce Coleman Inc./John S. Flannery, 18, 27 (middle left)
Corbis/Larry Edwards/ZUMA, 29
Dwight R. Kuhn, 4 (inset)
Jim Kalisch, University of Nebraska-Lincoln, Entomology, 8, 9, 26 (top right)
Nature Picture Library/Ingo Arndt, 6, 26 (top left)
Peter Arnold, Inc./David Scharf, cover
Photo Researchers, Inc./Bill Bachmann, 4 (main); Dr. Tony Brain, 24; Eye of Science,
    22; James H. Robinson, 14; Larry Mulvehill, 16 (bottom); Martin Dohrn, 23,
    27 (bottom left); Robert Noonan, 10, 26 (bottom left); Sinclair Stammers,
    21, 27 (middle right)
Robert McCaw, 16 (top), 27 (top right)
Visuals Unlimited/Bill Beatty, 15, 27 (top left); Doug Sokell, 12, 26 (bottom right);
    Larry Jensen, 11; Science VU/CDC, 25, 27 (bottom right)

TABLE OF CONTENTS

Dangerous Bugs...................... 4

Number 10........................... 6

Number 9............................ 8

Number 8............................ 10

Number 7............................ 12

Number 6............................ 14

Number 5............................ 16

Number 4............................ 18

Number 3............................ 20

Number 2............................ 22

Number 1............................ 24

Understanding Bugs 28

Glossary 30

Read More 31

Internet Sites. 31

Index. 32

DANGEROUS BUGS

Termite nests can be the size of a small house! But even these destructive bugs weren't nasty enough to make our top 10 list.

The thought of certain animals can stir fear in your heart. The grizzly bear. The great white shark. The rattlesnake.

Such animals are frightening, but others are far more threatening. Some of nature's most dangerous creatures buzz around people's ears, crawl on floors, and hide in corners. People call them pests. Creepy-crawlers. Bugs. Scientists know them as arthropods.

Bugs and the diseases they carry kill millions of people each year. They sicken or scar millions more.

But don't get so scared that you stop going outside. Only a few bugs are truly harmful. Most of them don't live in North America. Plus, not all dangerous bugs are killers. Some cause brief but breathtaking pain. Others just do disgusting things.

Now, go make sure your window screens are tightly closed. Then keep reading to learn about 10 nasty bugs.

10

The puss caterpillar's soft hairs hide stinging spines.

HABITAT: West to Texas and north to Maryland

ADULTHOOD: Moths covered with long hairs, called flannel moths

DEFENSE: Can pull its head almost completely into its body

FYI: Poison causes shocking pain that eases and returns in waves

PUSS CATERPILLAR

Caterpillars may look cute and harmless, but looks can be deceiving. Poisonous caterpillars live on four continents. About a dozen poisonous species live in North America. The puss caterpillar is a nasty one.

Puss caterpillars are covered with long red-brown hairs. Their coats appear fuzzy and soft. They look like the sort of creature a child might try to pet. But doing that would be a big mistake.

When frightened, puss caterpillars arch their backs like angry cats. Their hairs rise and reveal sharp spines. Each spine is connected to a poison-filled gland. The spine acts like a needle. It injects a burst of poison into anything it touches.

The poison causes burning pain, swelling, and numbness. In severe cases, it can cause high fever, vomiting, and paralysis. And that's no fun for anyone.

Human bot fly maggots are about 1 inch (2.5 centimeters) long.

HUMAN BOT FLY

What's under your skin? Maybe it's a human bot fly. If so, you could be dinner. The trouble begins when the bot flies reproduce. They look for a warm and moist place on a person's body to lay their eggs. Larvae, or maggots, hatch from the eggs and burrow into the skin.

The maggots feed on human tissue, often in the brain and eyes. The human host itches, swells, and breaks out in sores. Some victims vomit and have headaches. In rare cases, the person is left blind.

After 20 to 60 days, the maggots push from under the skin and drop to the ground. At that point, they molt into pupae. Soon, they are mature flies.

Surely more dangerous bugs exist, but the human bot fly could be the grossest.

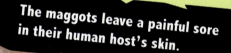

The maggots leave a painful sore in their human host's skin.

SIZE: Adult flies are 0.5 inches to 0.75 inches (1.3 to 1.9 centimeters) across.

HABITAT: Central and South America

FYI: Human bot flies sometimes attach their eggs to another insect, such as a mosquito or black fly. The insect lands on a human and deposits the eggs.

8 BROWN RECLUSE

The brown recluse often hides in woodpiles.

HABITAT: Mainly southern states, but are found north to Iowa and west to Texas

SIZE: Including the legs, about the size of a quarter

EYES: Six, unlike most other spiders, which have eight eyes

One type of brown recluse spider is common in the southern United States. This threatening spider often crawls into bedding or piled clothing.

When it bites, the brown recluse releases venom. This poison causes burning and stinging, along with vomiting and exhaustion. At first, the spider's venom blisters and blackens the skin. Then, it opens a sore that heals slowly, if at all. In extremely rare cases, brown recluse bites can be deadly.

Many brown recluse victims end up with a deep scar. It forever marks the place of the bite.

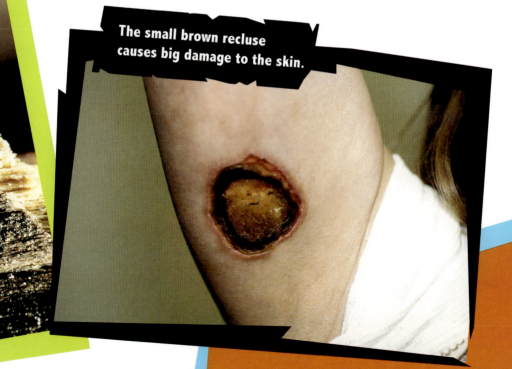

The small brown recluse causes big damage to the skin.

7

Scorpions have eight legs and a set of pincers.

SCORPION

At least 40 types of scorpions live in North America. One type is found as far north as Illinois.

Like spiders, scorpions are arachnids, which means they have eight legs. They also have a pair of crablike pincers in front and a dangerous stinger at the tip of the tail.

Scorpions hide in cracks and dark places. They feed on other bugs, lizards, mice, and even other scorpions. They use their poisonous sting on humans only rarely.

A scorpion sting causes burning pain. Victims drool, shake, and feel confused. They can suffer stomach cramps. The age of bite victims affects their risk. Children younger than 5 are far more likely to die from a scorpion bite than adults. But adults who are stung several times also face serious risks.

Size: 0.5 inch to 9 inches (1.3 centimeters to 23 centimeters) long

Food: Bugs, lizards, mice, and other scorpions

FYI: Newborn scorpions ride on their mothers' backs for their first two weeks of life.

5 BLACK WIDOW

A female black widow (bottom) is much larger than the male (top).

You do not want to come across a female black widow spider. Especially if you are a male black widow spider.

Black widows won their name from the female's habit of eating the male soon after mating. His death makes her a widow.

Female black widows have a red hourglass marking.

Female black widows release venom when they chomp into the skin of a human or other creature. The venom is 15 times as powerful as rattlesnake venom. Fortunately for their human victims, the amount of venom is too small to kill most people.

But victims endure horrible pain, rigid muscles, sweating, and breathing problems. The symptoms can go on for days. In four of every 100 cases, the victim never recovers.

SIZE: Females are about 1.5 inches (3.8 centimeters) long with legs extended; males are smaller.

HABITAT: Throughout North America; most common in the southern United States

FYI: Indoor plumbing helped decrease people's encounters with black widow spiders, which often lived in outhouses.

5

Body hairs look huge next to a tiny deer tick.

One of the first signs of Lyme disease is a rash that looks like a bull's-eye.

DEER TICK

Deer ticks are about the size of sesame seeds. You might not even notice one crawling on your skin.

The ticks prefer to fill up on the blood of deer or mice. But they sometimes bite other creatures, including humans. A deer tick will stay attached, drinking blood, for up to four days before falling off the host's body.

Each year, deer ticks infect thousands of people with Lyme disease. The disease begins with a rash around the tick bite. It looks like a bull's-eye. Early symptoms include headaches and fever. Later, victims may have stiff joints and heart problems. Few victims die, but their suffering can go on for years.

HABITAT: Most common in northeastern and midwestern states

FIRST OUTBREAK OF LYME DISEASE: Near Lyme, Connecticut, in 1977

TREATMENT OF LYME DISEASE: Antibiotics

4

APPEARANCE: Nearly identical to common honey bees

RANGE: Africanized bees will chase their victims for one-half mile (0.8 kilometer) or more.

FYI: The average person can survive 1,000 to 1,500 bee stings at one time.

AFRICANIZED BEE

One sting from an Africanized bee is nothing to worry about. It's no more dangerous than a sting from a common honey bee. The trouble is, Africanized bees don't give out stings in small numbers.

Africanized bees attack in swarms. Their victims may be stung thousands of times. That many stings can kill.

In 1957, a small group of African queen bees escaped from a lab in Brazil. They mated with local bees and created the more aggressive Africanized bees. They've been moving north ever since, reaching Texas in 1990.

Over the years, Africanized bees earned the nickname "killer bees." Their attacks have killed about 1,000 people in South America, Central America, and Mexico. In the United States, they're responsible for about 15 deaths.

3 KISSING BUG

Kissing bugs are anything but lovable. Also called assassin bugs, these insects drink the blood of sleeping people. Kissing bugs get their name because they often bite victims around the mouth and nose. Some types of kissing bugs have a painless bite. Other types have a bite that some experts believe is the most painful of any insect.

The real danger comes after the bite. Kissing bugs spread Chagas' disease. Some victims become sick right away. They suffer a rash, fever, and vomiting. Often, the skin near one eye will swell. Only a few of these victims die.

Other victims live for years with the disease lurking in their blood. They may experience heart and digestive problems 20 or 30 years after being bitten.

SIZE: About 0.75 inch (1.9 centimeters) long

HABITAT: Central and South America

DEATHS: About 50,000 people each year die from Chagas' disease.

21

The tsetse fly uses its needlelike mouthpart to feed on a victim's blood.

TSETSE FLY

One bite from a tsetse fly can put a person to sleep. For good.

Found only in Africa, the tsetse fly spreads a deadly disease known as sleeping sickness. Tsetse flies have a long, needlelike mouthpart. They use it to drink human blood.

As they drink, tsetse flies pass along a tiny parasite. The parasite infects the human nervous system. At first, victims feel like they have the flu. They run a fever and feel cold and tired. Soon, they lose all strength. Their brain swells, and they become cranky and confused. They then fall into a coma. Thousands never awaken.

As the tsetse fly drinks, it injects the parasite that causes sleeping sickness.

SIZE: Slightly larger than a housefly

HABITAT: Africa

THREATS: About 100,000 people get sleeping sickness every year.

FYI: Females lay one egg at a time. Other types of flies lay as many as 250 eggs at once.

23

1 MOSQUITO

The female *Anopheles gambiae* mosquito carries malaria.

TYPES: At least 2,400 types worldwide; about 100 types are found in North America

DEATHS: About 1 million each year

U.S. CASES: About 1,300 people in the United States get malaria each year. Almost all of them are infected while visiting other countries.

FYI: Only female mosquitoes bite. They need blood in order to produce eggs.

As it drinks, a mosquito's abdomen fills with its victim's blood.

Most people would agree that mosquitoes are among the most annoying bugs in the world. But many people don't realize the real danger of the pest buzzing around their ears.

Mosquitoes spread many diseases, including yellow fever, West Nile virus, and encephalitis. But the greatest threat comes from malaria. As they bite, mosquitoes inject a small amount of saliva into their victim's blood. Some mosquitoes' saliva contains the parasite that causes malaria.

Each year, malaria infects about 300 million people across Africa, South America, and Asia. It destroys blood cells and clogs the flow of blood. Most deaths occur in Africa, where a child dies from malaria every 30 seconds.

No other bug or animal kills as many people.

The World's Most

DANGEROUS

BUGS

10

PUSS CATERPILLAR

9

HUMAN BOT FLY

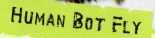

BROWN RECLUSE SPIDER

8

7

SCORPION

Black Widow Spider

6

5

Deer Tick

Africanized Bee

4

3

Kissing Bug

2

Tsetse Fly

Mosquito

1

UNDERSTANDING BUGS

Bugs are important. They help people survive. They keep the world running. How? Bugs provide food for other animals. They pollinate plants. They feed on dead plants and animals.

About 1 million known species of insects live on earth. And that number does not even include spiders and other arachnids. Experts believe there are millions more bugs that remain unknown and unnamed. Only a tiny number of bugs threaten humans.

Sure, bugs can be dangerous. The 10 described in this book cause much human suffering. But we can take steps to avoid these dangers. And we can learn to recognize bugs that pose no threat. Those bugs deserve our respect.

Scientists study bugs to learn about the environment.

Glossary

arachnid (uh-RAK-nuhd)—a small animal with eight legs, two body sections, and no wings or antennas

arthropod (AR-thruh-pod)—an animal with a hard outer shell and many legs with joints

larva (LAR-vuh)—an insect at the stage after an egg; more than one larva are larvae.

maggot (MAG-uht)—the wormlike larva of some flies

parasite (PAIR-uh-site)—an animal or plant that lives on or inside another animal or plant

pupa (PYOO-puh)—an insect at the stage of development between a larva and an adult; more than one pupa are pupae.

species (SPEE-sheez)—a group of plants or animals with similar features

venom (VEN-uhm)—poisonous liquid produced by animals such as spiders and scorpions

READ MORE

Houghton, Sarah. *Bloodsuckers: Bats, Bugs, and Other Bloodthirsty Creatures*. High Five Reading. Bloomington, Minn.: Red Brick Learning, 2004.

Stewart, Melissa. *Maggots, Grubs, and More: The Secret Lives of Young Insects*. Brookfield, Conn.: Millbrook Press, 2003.

Wilkes, Angela. *Dangerous Creatures*. Kingfisher Knowledge. New York: Kingfisher, 2003.

INTERNET SITES

FactHound offers a safe, fun way to find Internet sites related to this book. All of the sites on FactHound have been researched by our staff.

Here's how:

1. Visit *www.facthound.com*
2. Type in this special code **0736854568** for age-appropriate sites. Or enter a search word related to this book for a more general search.
3. Click on the **Fetch It** button.

FactHound will fetch the best sites for you!

INDEX

Africanized bee, 18–19
appearance, 7, 13, 18, 22
arachnids, 10–11, 12–13,
       14–15, 28

benefits, 28
black widow spider, 14–15
brown recluse spider, 10–11

deer tick, 16–17
diseases, 5
  Chagas' disease, 20, 21
  encephalitis, 25
  Lyme disease, 17
  malaria, 24, 25
  sleeping sickness, 22–23
  West Nile virus, 25
  yellow fever, 25

human bot fly, 8–9

kissing bug, 20–21

maggots, 8–9
mosquito, 9, 24–25

parasites, 23, 25
poison, 6, 7, 11, 13
pupae, 9
puss caterpillar, 6–7

scorpion, 12–13
size, 9, 10, 13, 15, 17, 21, 23

tsetse fly, 22–23

venom, 11, 15